Be Credit*WIZE*

Tips, Tools, and Tactics
for Controlling
Your Credit

Starting TODAY!!!

BeCreditWize.com

Carol DeMarco

Cover designed by Lindsay Powell.

First published by Dog Ear Publishing
4011 Vincennes Rd
Indianapolis, IN 46268
www.dogearpublishing.net

ISBN: 978-1-4575-3678-6

This book is printed on acid-free paper.

Printed in the United States of America

ACKNOWLEDGEMENTS

I want to give special thanks to all of those potential borrowers who opened their financial lives to me through the years. Their trust and inspiration have lead me to where I am today.

I also want to thank those around me who have believed in me and have encouraged me to create this book…you know who you are.

And, lastly, I am forever grateful for my faith and the guidance I have received from it…Thanks, Mom, for giving me that gift.

Table of Contents

Foreword

During my 20+-year career in the credit industry, I helped hundreds of people achieve the American dream of home ownership. Some were easy, some, not so much. What I realized during those years was that no matter what one's background, education, or profession, there was a universal thread that wound through almost every borrower's financial background...***confusion about personal credit!*** Often people were frustrated because they did not understand how past financial decisions may have radically affected their credit scores. Just a few missteps often caused roadblocks that stood in the way of their having the power to create their best lives. The information provided herein is intended to help you avoid some of those mistakes, repair previous problems and to maintain control of your financial future.

This book offers facts regarding what credit is and how to control it. I want the readers of this book to realize that credit is factual entity. It is NOT emotional! Thus, it can be controlled. It is my belief that anything that is factually based can be controlled with dedication, patience, and knowledge. As the author, I do not intend to act as a credit counselor, but to offer information that will <u>increase your knowledge and understanding of credit.</u>

The adage that Knowledge is Power is so true with regard to the subject of credit. The knowledge you will gain with this book will provide the roadmap to your ***credit independence***.

Keep reading and become
credit empowered!

CHAPTER 1

Ever wish that you knew more about your credit report?

You are not alone!

Credit reports and credit scores are among the most important, confusing, irritating and yet personal parts of our lives. The emotional connection to our credit report can result in embarrassment, anger or pride, depending on what shape our credit is in at any point in time. We know we should understand more about what influences our credit scores, but, where do we turn for reliable AND comprehensible information? The credit reporting agencies and lenders typically do not provide much assistance. Our schools and colleges do not provide credit curriculum. Our families and friends are often as uninformed about credit as we are. And, most of the books that are available are confusing and will put us right to sleep! However, here we are going to take the mystery out of your credit report and have some fun! Let's get started...*FIRST*...

What is CREDIT?

Credit is the use of someone

else's money with the

expectation of timely repayment

plus interest.

Why should we care about credit?

CREDIT can affect where you **Live**

CREDIT can affect where you **Work**

CREDIT can affect what you can **Afford**

CREDIT can affect your borrowing **Power**

CREDIT can affect your **Image**

CREDIT can affect your **Well-Being**

How?
Let's *take a look....*

Credit can affect...

Where You Live

- Most potential landlords will check your previous pay history

- All mortgage companies will check your previous pay history

- The better your previous pay history, the better your housing can be

Where You Work

- Many potential employers will check your credit

- Credit can appear to be an indicator of self-management

- Credit can be perceived as a representation of one's stability

- Credit can appear as an indicator of personal organization

- Credit management can be regarded as an indication of financial understanding

All of these items could affect

a potential employer's judgment

of job performance.

What You Can Afford

- Poor credit ratings will result in higher interest rates if and when credit is issued.

- The higher the interest rate, the higher your payment, therefore the less you can afford.

- The lower the interest rate, the lower your payment, therefore the more you can afford.

Your Borrowing Power

The more effectively you manage your credit, the more borrowing power you will have to

- Purchase a car

- Start a business

- Own a home

- Go to college

Your Image

- Your credit can be interpreted as a direct reflection of how you manage your financial life.

- Your credit is a factual picture of your past self-control.

- Others may see inconsistent or sloppy credit as representative of the rest of your behavior.

Your Well-Being

Poor Credit can contribute to

- Poor Self-image

- Lack of Confidence

- Health Problems

- Stress

WIZE Thoughts

Credit effects your life in almost every way.

You must manage your credit

If not now, When?

CHAPTER 2

Credit, A Key Component of Financial Literacy

Why is *Credit Literacy* so Important?

Most people have a checking account and have a good understanding of how it works.

Most people have used a debit card and have a pretty good understanding of how it works.

Most people have a credit card (or two) and have some understanding of how they work.

Most people know about budgets and may have a little understanding of how they work.

However...

Few really know much about Credit

or

how it impacts their lives.

Many have never seen their credit report.

Few understand what impacts their credit scores.

Few know that where they work, where they live, and even their overall well-being is impacted by their credit management skills.

Many think of credit as a *MYSTERIOUS* item
over which they have no control.

NOT TRUE!

Credit is Factual

Many people can become very emotional when it comes to their credit.   However, credit itself is not emotional at all. It is a listing of facts that have been reported electronically from a lender to a credit-reporting agency. The information is simply an account of one's borrowing behavior.

There is nothing on a credit report that says someone is a good or bad person. All that is reported is how a person pays their bills.

Thus, anything that is factual can be controlled. Battling an OPINION of your credit behavior would be challenging, but with a credit report facts are facts, and one can control the facts by managing their financial behavior.

Reporting mistakes may occur; however, those too can be managed by correcting them.

It is paramount that one never feels that one is a victim of poor credit reporting; after all, facts are facts, and it is up to you to control them. If you don't like what is reflected on your credit report, commit to changing it.

With accurate information and dedication, you can be in complete control of your credit.

Understanding your credit report and how it can
be managed
is a powerful step toward a better quality of life.

Remember....

- Good credit starts slowly and builds over time

- Negative credit can be reversed over time with knowledge and commitment

- Established credit must be continually monitored and controlled.The better your credit history, the less interest you will pay.

- The poorer your credit history, the more interest you will pay.

WIZE Thoughts

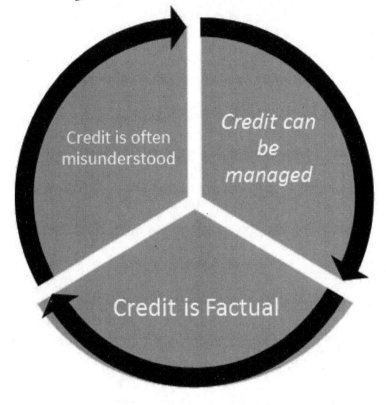

CHAPTER 3

Let's Talk About Interest

Interest is the cost of borrowing money.

- Interest is determined partly by market conditions.

- Interest rates are determined primarily by the lender's analysis of how you will repay based upon your past credit history.

- Interest is calculated as a percentage of the loan amount.

- Interest is charged in addition to the borrowed amount.

- Interest will be paid in periodic increments and is normally included in monthly payments.

- Interest is the primary component of a lender's profit when lending money.

More on Interest...

- Lending sources—such as banks, credit unions, and credit cards— are in business to be profitable.

- Interest = profit to the lending source

- Lenders create profit in many ways, but their primary source is the interest they charge on borrowed money.

Interest:
How is it calculated?

Simple interest and amortized interest are the two most commonly used calculations. Amortized interest is typically used when financing a home. Often simple interest is used when financing a car .

Example #1 Financing your new car.

Simple Interest: interest calculated as a simple percentage of the original principal (loan) amount

Example: 48-month loan
$25,000 loan amount @ 4.5% interest
4.5 x 25000 = $1125 interest per year

Interest = $93.75 due / month

Principal and Interest payment:

$25,000 / 48 months =

Principal = $520.00 due/month

Total payment = $613.75 per month

<u>*Example #2 Financing your new home.*</u>

<u>*Amortization Interest*</u>: interest collected monthly, and amount paid as interest decreases over the term of the loan. The interest rate may be fixed or variable for the life of the loan.

Example: 30-year mortgage loan
$100,000 loan amount @ 4.5% interest =
$504.00 / month including interest and principal reduction

Month 1 = $504.00 total payment
$375.00 interest
$129.00 principal reduction
New principal balance: $100,000 - $129.00 = $99,871

Month 2 = $504.00 total payment
$374.51 interest
$129.49 principal reduction
New principal balance: $99,871 - 129.49 = $99,741.60

Each month the interest payment is a little less and payment to the principal is a little more. The overall monthly payment stays the same; only the distribution changes monthly.

See appendix for typical amortization schedule

How Are Interest Rates Determined?

Interest rates are determined somewhat by market factors over which you have no control.

The single largest factor that a lender utilizes in determining your interest rate is your prior credit history.

If the lender sees that you have paid previous commitments slowly, they may determine that you will pay them in a similar manner, therefore, your interest rate will be higher.

Likewise, if the lender sees that you have paid previous commitments on time, they will probably determine that you will pay them in a similar manner, therefore, your interest rate will be lower.

**The higher the interest rate,
the higher your monthly payment will be
and the less you can afford...**

Think about the following examples:

How MUCH Can You AFFORD
Per Month?

Different interest rates will give you different monthly payments. Here are some examples of what you might be paying.

(For these examples, excellent credit is considered to be over 700 and poor credit is under 620. More on these number later.)

Home Loan

$100,000 Loan

Excellent Credit Interest Rate: 4.5%

$504.79 / month payment*

$100,000 Loan

Poor credit interest rate:

7.5%

$694.87/ month payment**

An amortized payment is determined by plugging the original loan balance into a formula that will accomplish total payoff of that amount over the term of the loan, typically 30 years.

**If you want to maintain a payment of $504.79 per month but must pay the higher interest rate, your maximum loan amount could be only $68,000, not $100,000.

Either way, you can now see that you may be able to afford a home of your own for no more than what you are paying in rent!

Auto Loan

Again, different interest rates will give you different monthly payments. Here are some examples of what you might be paying.

$25,000

Excellent credit interest rate: 2.5%

$546.00 / month payment

Poor credit interest rate: 8.5%

$611.00 / month payment*

*If you want to maintain a payment of $546.00 per month, but, must pay the higher interest rate, your maximum loan amount could be only $21,000.

Credit Card

Wildly differing interest rates here can cause untold financial burdens. Read the fine print and shop around.

Not all credit cards are created equal!

$5000 Balance

Good Credit: 8.5% Interest

$35.00/month interest

Plus a nominal principal payment

Poor Credit: 25% Interest

$150.00/month interest*

Plus a nominal principal payment

*It can take up to 12 years to pay off this balance making minimum required payments at this interest rate.

How much will you pay
over the
Life of the Loan?

Home Loan

$100,000 @ 4.5% Interest

30 years

Total Cost = $181,725

(4.5 X $100,000 x 30 years)

$100,000 @7.5% Interest

30 years

Total Cost = $250,153

(7.5 X $100,000 x 30 years)

With the higher interest (resulting from a lower credit score), you will pay $68,428 more!

Auto Loan

$25,000

@2.5% interest = $26,208 over 4 years

2.5 X $25,000 x 4 years

@7.5% interest = $29,320 over 4 years

7.5 X $25,000 x 4 years

At the higher interest rate, you will pay _$3,112_ more!

Credit Card

$5000

@ 8.5% interest= $850

Over 24 months

@ 25% interest = $2500

Over 24 months

Again, at the higher interest rate, you will pay LOTS more!

You can now see how the amount of interest you are charged determines how much you will pay for many items you may need for everyday life.

You also now know that the interest you will be charged is based on your previous credit history.

Now, let's discuss how the lender reviews
your previous credit performance—
on your CREDIT REPORT

WIZE Thoughts

Interest is a key factor in determining your total monthly payment.

Interest is profit for the lending institution.

Interest rates are determined primarily by the lender's analysis of how you will repay based on your past credit history.

CHAPTER 4

What About Credit Reports?

What is a Credit Report?

A credit report is the written summary of the manner in which you manage your borrowing habits.

- The better you manage your credit performance the more favorable your report will be.

- Any company from which you have obtained credit can place information on your credit report regarding your financial repayment performance.

- Reported items can be credit cards, car loans, home loans, auto leases, department store accounts, etc.

What is on a Credit Report?

Personal Information

- Name
- Address
- Social security number
- Marital status
- Employer
- Previous credit
- Inquiries
- Public records

Creditors

- Company name
- Loan number
- Dates of loan
- Amounts of loans
- Payment amounts
- Late payment dates
- Current loan status

What is
not
on a
Credit Report?

Typically not reported

- Cell Phone

- Rent

- Child support

- Child care

- Insurance

- Home phone

- INCOME

HOWEVER, if you do not pay on time,
these companies may report the negative information.

WHO COMPILES ALL THE INFORMATION?

Below are the three agencies to whom all of your
creditors may report your credit information.
Although each is independent of the others,
the information reported is similar.

Experian

P.O. box 2104
Allen, Texas 75132
(888) Experian
(397-3742)
www.experian/help.com

Equifax

P.O. box 740241
Atlanta, Georgia 30374
(800) 685-1111
www.equifax.com\FCRA

Transunion

P.O. box 2000
Chester, Pennsylvania 29011
(800) 680-7289
www.transunion.com

Note, this information is also included in the appendix.

How is your credit connected to
YOU??

Your credit and you...
(and <u>only</u> you)

All reported information is driven to your credit report via your

Social Security Number.

Your Social Security Number is
unique to you; it is your

<u>Financial Fingerprint</u>.

With that
Financial Fingerprint...

- Companies may send your borrowing history to the three bureaus (Experian, Equifax, Transunion)

- Companies can view your entire credit report online

- **Thieves can become you!**

Your Social Security Number is unique to you, so it must be treated with respect and protected from misuse.

Your
Credit Report,
Your
Financial Blueprint

- It represents your credit behavior

- It represents you to new creditors,
  who have nothing else to go on

- It must be periodically reviewed for accuracy

Remember, you must grant permission to a potential creditor to review your credit report. However, new creditors will almost never grant new credit without reviewing your past credit behavior as reported on our credit report.

What Does a Credit Report Look Like?

There are multiple report formats, however, most contain the same information.

Let's take a look...

Section by Section

The following credit report represents a merged accounting of information provided by the three credit bureaus, Transunion, Experian and Equifax.

There are many formats used in the world of credit reporting, however, they all contain the same general information. The format used is one of the most comprehensive examples.

Personal Data

EFX, XPN, TU = Equifax, Experian, Transunion

Big Credit Mortgage	Order:	463538
1234 Anywhere Drive	Repository:	EFX,XPN,TU
NY,NY 32222	Date Requested:	July 22, 2014
PH: 212-444-5555	Loan Number:	23499608

Prepared For

ABC Bank	Report Type: INDIVIDUAL
789 Main Street	Price: $10.00
Jacksonville, FL 32259	Account Number: 0087947734
	Ordered By: CD

Borrower Information

Name:	Judy Borrower
Social Security Number:	123-34-4567
Address	4000 E. Anywhere Dr. 34567
Marital Status:	Married

Your current information

Company requesting report

Credit Scores

This is where it all begins...*or ends*...!

Shortcut...Credit Scores are the first thing that lenders look at when beginning the lending process. Why? The credit profile has already been analyzed by the credit scoring formulas...the Lender's job is practically done for them! But, don't tell them that!

Credit Score			
	Judy Borrower		EFX
	00001	Amount on available too high	
669 Beacon	00002	Too many open revolving accounts	
	00005	Too many revolving accounts	
	Judy Borrower		XPN
622 Fair Isaac	01	Current balances too high	
	02	Too many revolving accounts	
	04	Too few installment accounts	
	05	Delinquent accounts reporting	
	Judy Borrower		TU
634 FICO	001	High balances outstanding	
	002	Delinquencies	
	003	High balances to available credit	
	004	Lack of installment credit	

One score form each bureau

Reason codes for score calculations

Alerts

Any comment here may be questioned during the loan process.

Alerts

Judy 238-40-0000

Risk Score Value – Equifax was adversely impacted by recent credit inquiries

Address Discrepancy – address provided different from data.

SAFESCAN Warning – Social Security Number issued within the last 4 years*

*Possible reasons: recent immigrant, witness protection, erroneous date input, fraud, etc.

WHAT?

WHY?

Credit Summary

Summary of all report entries.

The second area on the credit report that Lenders review.

Credit Summary

Acct Type	#	# / Bal	Total Bal.	Total Pmt	Total 30	60	90	Late Date
Real Estate	2	2	$445,435	$ 2222	1	1	0	4/2010
Install	2	2	$ 16,454	$ 575	1	0	0	4/2015
Revolving	2	1	$ 944	$ 97	0	0	0	
Collection	0	0	0	0	0	0	0	
Other	0	0	0	0	0	0	0	
Total	4	5	$462,833	$ 2894	2	1	0	

Public Records	Liens	Judgements	Foreclosure	Bankruptcy	Other	Total
	1	1	0	1	0	3

Total Inquiries   4   Total Past Due $ 575

What's this?

All of these negative items will
require explanations to the lender.

Creditor Entries

Lender	Date Opened	Latest DT Reported	Account Type	ECOA	High Credit	Balance	Past Due Amount	Current Rating	Dt Last Active
Any Bank 080875	2007-08	2014-08	Mortgage	Joint	384,000	244,425		1	

Pay Pattern	Pay Pattern Start Date	Adverse Dates	Source	Monthly Payment	Terms	Months Reviewed	30-60-90
Ccccccccccc	2013/07	▼	TU, EFX, XPN	2229	360 mo	36	-0-

Loan Type: Conv Mortgage
Comments: Current Acct.

Perfect!

Lender	Date Opened	Latest DT Reported	Account Type	ECOA	High Credit	Balance	Past Due Amount	Current Rating	Dt Last Active
ALERT									
Car Credit Company 897974	2012-12	2014-06	Install	Joint	35000	15454	875	2	2014-04

Pay Pattern	Pay Pattern Start Date	Adverse Dates	Source	Monthly Payment	Terms	Months Reviewed	30-60-90
Ccccccccc-ccccccc-cc	2012-12	2014-03 2013-06 2012-12	EFX, TU	.875	48 mo	17	3

Loan Type: AUTO
Comments: Currently Past Due

OOPS...late!

Every Credit account, active and inactive is listed individually within the body of the credit report. And ACTIVE accounts are included in the Credit Summary outlined on the previous page.

Public Records

A Public Record is any recorded account information that a governmental body, such as a county, is required to maintain on file and which must be accessible by the public. This includes the files of most legal actions such as collections, judgements, liens, bankruptcies and foreclosures.

Public Records

Public records have been checked for legal actions including judgments and bankruptcies reported on the subject and/or spouse from TU/XPN/EFX

Name	Record Type	Source	Amount	Court	Date Recorded	Date Settled*
Judy Borrower 34734	Tax Lien	TU	28434	Orange County	2007 06	2008 11
Type: Federal Tax Lien						
Judy Borrower 37211	Bankruptcy Chapter 7	TU, EFX	72748	Orange County	2009 04	2010 01
Type: Voluntary Bankruptcy, Chapter 7						
Judy Borrower	Judgment	TU	1840	Orange County	2009 04	2010 01
Type Judgment including in Bankruptcy						

*This date starts the clock to recovery.

*County, State and Federal records are searched for recorded public records.
*Legal action documents may be recorded in the county in which the event occurred or in the county of residence at the time of the event.

Borrower Address

And

Employment

Borrower and Co Borrower address Information		
Address	Borrower/CoBorrower	Source
1234 Anywhere , USA 34332	B/C	TU,EXP
1234 Anywhere, USE 34332	B/C	EXP
3455 There, USA 55555	C	TU

Borrower/CoBorrower Employment Address Information		
Big Time Company, Duluth, MN	B	T

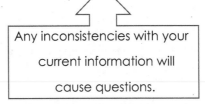

Any inconsistencies with your current information will cause questions.

All information submitted via the new loan application must match the information contained here. If it does not, be prepared to explain the discrepancies.

Inquiries

An inquiry is recorded any time a potential or current creditor reviews your credit report.

Credit Inquiries			
Inquiring Company Name	Inquiry Date	Borrower/Coborrower	Regulatory
Car Company	2013/04	B	EFX/TU
Car Company	2013/05	C	TU
Dept. Store	2013/06	B	EFX

Too many of these entries will lower your score.

All companies who request your credit report will be reported here. The inquiry will typically appear for 6 months.

Additionally, if you are car or mortgage shopping, all inquiries from the same type of Lender (car dealers or mortgage companies) within a 30 day period will typically be considered as only one "hit" to your credit score. However, if you apply for a car, a credit card and a mortgage, your score will be reduced three times...as much as 15 points for each instance! These reductions will occur if you do or do not receive the loan. So, apply for credit sparingly.

File Variations

Any variation may require an explanation
during the loan process. Maiden names,
previous addresses, etc., will require explanations.

File Variations			
Regulatory	Name	SS#	Birth Date
B / TU	Judy Borrower	123-45-6789	04/30/1964
B / TU, EFX	Judy P Borrower	123-45-6789	04/30/1964
B / EPN	Judy P Mason	123-45-6879	04/30/1965
Comments			
Equifax	Name Discrepancy		
Transunion	Name Discrepancy		
Equifax	Address differs from Inquiry		
Experian	Name Discrepancy		
Experian	SS# does not match SS# in file		
Experian	Birth Date differs from Inquiry		

Discrepancies noted here are the
result of comparing the current
credit application and previous
information in the existing credit profile.
Be prepared to explain the differences.
Many are caused by simple human error,
but, others may be a red flag
alerting the lender – and you – to possible
fraud.

Creditor Contact Information

Use this information to
contact your creditors.

Creditor				
Creditor Name	Acct #	Address	Phone	Creditor Code
Credit card Co.	xxxxx	4301#M Street Memphis, TN 34076	3849874892	xxxx
Car Company	xxxxx	84900 X Street Detroit, MI 38978	4808082893	xxxx
That Bank	xxxxx	223 Y Street Anywhere, USA 38970	9889902903	xxxx
Mortgage Co.	xxxxx	123 H Street Birmingham, AL 33478	3877838048	xxxx

Credit Bureau Information		
Transunion, LLC P.O. Box 1000 Chester, PA 19022 866-877-2673 Transunion.com	Equifax Information Svc, LLC P.O. Box 7490241 Atlanta, GA 30374 800-685-1111 Equifax.com	Experian Credit 701 Experian Pkwy P.O. Box 2002 Allen, TX 75013 888-397-3742 Experian.com

Communication is your best tool for keeping your credit report accurate and free from erroneous information. If you see something that does not seem right to you, do not ignore it. Believe it or not, lenders want to provide accurate information regarding their customers. However, it is YOUR responsibility to hold them accountable. Communicate, communicate, communicate.

Start with the credit bureaus. Challenge information that you do not think is correct. They are required to check it out on your behalf. But, your direct contact with the creditor is always a good idea. And, once you have made that first request for corrections... follow up until you know the reported information is correct.

O.F.A.C

Office of Foreign Assets Control

The O.F.A.C office performs oversight of governmental agencies activities involving financial transactions.

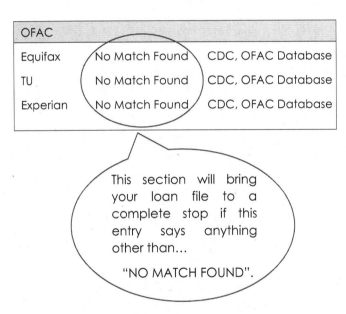

This section will bring your loan file to a complete stop if this entry says anything other than...

"NO MATCH FOUND".

If your information is linked with any found on a government watch list, "Match Found" will appear.

The following tables contain explanations
of codes used in the previous credit report sections.

ECOA Explanations

Equal Credit Opportunity Act

The ECOA regulation was implemented in the early 1970's. Its basic purpose is to prohibit lenders from refusing credit to anyone on the basis of anything but one's creditworthiness. One's sex, race, religion, etc., are not considered part of their creditworthiness, but, only their ability to repay based on more financial information. The codes below were designed within the regulation to make a credit report easier to interpret and thus help to protect the consumer from unfair credit practices.

ECOA Codes	Description
A	**Authorized User** – This is an authorized user of this account; another individual has contracted responsibility
B	**On Behalf of Another Person** – The subject has financial responsibility for an account that is used exclusively by another person
C	**Co-maker** – The subject has co-signed for a loan and will be responsible for payment if the borrower should default
I	**Individual Account** – The subject of the report has contracted responsibility for this account and is primarily responsible for its payment
J	**Joint Account** – The subject and another person (or persons) are jointly responsible for the payment on this account
M	**Maker** – The subject is responsible for payment of a loan, but a co-maker will be responsible for payment if maker defaults
P	**Participant Account** – borrower participates in a shared account whom cannot be distinguished as a co-maker or an authorized user
S	**Shared Account** – creditor knows that borrower and at least one other person share the account, but not enough information is given to designate as a joint or authorized user account
T	**Terminated Account** – borrower's relations with account has ended, although other parties who once shared the account with borrower may continue to maintain the account
U	**Undesignated Account** – creditor did not indicate who is responsible for the account
X	**Deceased**

Account Rating Codes

The following codes are used to help the consumer and lenders better understand information provided on a credit report. The codes are used by all of the credit bureaus. The codes indicate past behavior of that account.

Rating/Status Codes	Rating Description
0	Too new to rate; approved but not used, or unknown
1	Pays within 30 days of due date
2	Pays between 31 to 60 days, or is 2 payments past due
3	Pays between 61 to 90 days, or is 3 payments past due
4	Pays between 91 to 120 days, or is 4 payments past due
5	Pays over 120 Days, or is more than 4 payments past due
6	Included in Bankruptcy, chapter 13 type
8	Repossession
9	Charge off
Blank	No Rate reported

Account Status Codes

The following codes are used to help the consumer and lenders better understand information provided on a credit report. The codes are used by all of the credit bureaus. The codes indicate current status of that account.

Rating/Status Code	Status Description
A	Lost or stolen card
C	Contact member for status
D	Refinanced or renewed
E	Consumer deceased
F	In financial counseling
G	Foreclosure process started
J	Adjustment pending
M	Included in Chapter 13
S	Dispute — resolution pending
Z	Included in bankruptcy
$	Assigned to US Department of Education
W	Need consumer authorization
X	No record of account

WIZE Thoughts

Your Social Security Number is yours and yours alone.

Your Credit Report tells so much about you.

YOUR JOB is to keep your Credit Report Accurate.

CHAPTER 5

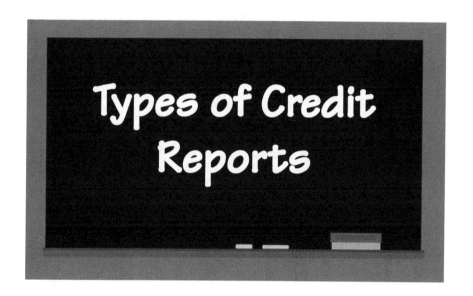

Types of Credit Reports

There are four types of credit report profiles.

- Individual
- Joint with Spouse
- Individual Without Spouse
- Joint with Non-spouse

#1 Individual

This report will contain credit listed in only one name, plus any accounts on which you have jointly borrowed.

Two or more non-spouse individuals who are applying for new credit will have each report pulled as individuals, even if the new loan will be in multiple names. All debts and credit scores will be included in the credit decision.

A married person may obtain credit without their spouse. Only the borrower's credit, income, and assets will be used for approval.*

In many states, a non-borrowing spouse will have ownership rights to the couple's primary residence even though they are not liable for the debt. Those states are said to have Homestead Laws.

#2 Joint with Spouse

This report will contain credit listed individually for each spouse as well as any accounts on which both spouses are jointly liable.

A joint report may be pulled for married couples. Unmarried couples will have individual reports pulled. Some companies will request a joint report for couples with Civil Union status if their state does not yet allow same sex marriage.

When obtaining joint credit, all income and assets may be combined for approval. However, all debts for both spouses must be considered.

In many states, although both Spouses are obligated on the debt, the collateral may be in the name of only one spouse.

#3 Individual Without Spouse

This report will be pulled if a married person is applying for debt without their spouse joining on the loan. Only the income, assets, and debts of the borrowing spouse will be considered for approval.

A spouse may still have ownership rights to collateral even if not obligated on the debt, typically on primary residence.*

In many states, a non-borrowing spouse will have ownership rights to the couple's primary residence even though they are not liable for the debt. Those states are said to have Homestead Laws.

#4 Joint with Non-spouse

This type will be used when two or more non-married individuals apply for a loan.

Individual credit reports will be pulled and reviewed. Debt, income, and credit scores for all applicants will be considered for qualification.

In this instance, both borrowers must be on title to the collateral to maintain ownership but not to be liable for the debt.*

This type of borrowing may also be called "cosigning"

Adding a co-borrower may assist with qualifying for a loan, but their good credit will NOT compensate for the poor credit of the other borrower.

Guidelines for ownership between non-spouses vary by state.

Special Note:
<u>Cosigners</u>

- *A cosigner enters into a debt equally with another borrower.*

- *A cosigner may be a non-spousal borrower or relative for <u>jointly</u> owned collateral*

- *A cosigner may be a non-spousal borrower or relative for <u>non-jointly</u> owned collateral*

- *All credit activity is reported equally, so failure to repay the debt in an "as agreed" manner will negatively affect the credit of BOTH borrowers equally.*

- *Typically, account correspondence will be sent to one address only.*

Before you agree to become a co-signor or you request that someone become one for you, be confident that all parties fully understand the consequences. Becoming a co-signor can be a generous step...just protect yourself by understanding what can happen. Trusting your loved one is great, but, just be aware.

WIZE Thoughts

There are many ways to borrow.

Your borrowing can effect others.

PROTECT your borrowing power.

CHAPTER 6

Now, Let's Talk About Credit Scores

Credit Scores

Your Creditworthiness at a Glance

What is a
Credit Score?

Credit Scores are numeric indicators of current and past credit activity as compared to a *Perfect Model*.

Facts About Credit Scores

- Scores are assigned by each of the three credit bureaus based on their specific, yet similar, models

- How the numeric formulas work is unique to each bureau and are not published

- Scores range from 350 – 850

- Models are based on millions of credit profiles with perfect payment performance

- The best performing profiles are assigned the highest credit scores

- The closer your data compares to the model, the higher your score will be

- Lending theory supports that the higher your score, the more likely you are to make your payments on time in the future

- Accepted guidelines usually support that past payment patterns are an accurate predictor of future performance

Credit Scoring
Five Key Factors

A credit score is the result of a mathematical calculation.

There are five components of the formula used to calculate a credit score.*

They will now be revealed to you!

> *Payment Pattern*................*35%*
> *Outstanding Balance*.........*30%*
> *Length of Credit*...............*15%*
> *New Credit*.........................*10%*
> *Types of Credit*.................*10%*

Manage these and watch your credit score soar!
Let's examine each key...

*Each of the three credit bureaus have unique scoring methods. However, the percentages assigned to each of the **Five Key Factors** are all the same.

Key #1
Payment Pattern
35%

Definition: Do you pay debt as agreed?

Paying a debt by the date due is the most heavily weighted portion of a credit score. Following are some additional facts surrounding due dates and payment patterns.

- Re-Payment requirements are disclosed in loan documents and agreed to by you.

- Loan terms and disclosures should include monthly payment, payment date, commencement date, and loan term.

- With your signature, you agree to comply with these terms.

- Monthly payments are to be received by the creditor by the due date to avoid late fees.

- Late payments are reportable to the credit bureaus when payment is not received within 30 days after the due date, although late fees may be assessed earlier.

- One 30-day late payment can drop a credit score by 20-30 points overnight.

- It could take 12 months for your score to fully recover from just one 30 day late payment.

Key #2
Amounts Owed
30%

Definition: Actual Loan balance as compared to maximum credit available

This information contributes 30% to a credit score. A well balanced credit file is a bit trickier to accomplish and is probably the least known fact regarding a score. Below are some interesting yet little known facts about this key.

- Each debt has a maximum loan amount disclosed in the original loan agreement. Credit card limits may be increased over time. However, notification is always sent when increases are issued. The highest limit is also listed on a credit report under each creditor. This type of debt is called "Open Ended."

- The closer your outstanding balance is to the maximum credit amount available, the lower your credit score can be.

- Exceeding the maximum available limits can negatively impact your credit score by as much as 100 points.

- Best credit ratings have outstanding balances of less than 30% of available credit.

- For instance, if the maximum available credit card balance is $1000, keep the outstanding balance to less than $300.

- Contrary to popular belief, it is better to have more credit cards, each having a lower outstanding balance to maximum available ratio than one card with a very high balance-to-available ratio.

- It is thought that high balance-to-maximum ratios indicate a lack of good credit management. If you owe a certain dollar amount on one credit card that takes you to 80% of the maximum available credit, your score will suffer. However, if you owe the very same dollar amount on 3 seperate cards that show no more than 30% of the maximum available on each, your score will be higher. Additionally, some credit card companies will allow you to actually exceed your maximum available balance...if you MUST have those special shoes! BUT, exceeding the maximum available can cost your credit score up to 100 points over night!

Also

Do not close old accounts as they may strengthen your profile by adding age as well as a low balance to available ratio. Typically, an open credit card account with a zero balance will not hurt your score.

Key #3
Age of Credit
15%

Definition: How long your credit profile has been established?

Credit history is what all potential lenders look for on a credit report. A potential lender wants to see good credit management over time. Thus, when being calculated, a credit score also takes the age of a credit item into consideration. Here are some additional thoughts to consider.

- Newly obtained credit is necessary to get started

- Multiple yet modest credit balances will build higher scores more quickly than one large debt

- Re-activated old credit accounts will count as long-established accounts even if not used because the "date opened" date is the important part

- When starting an entirely new credit profile, alternative credit* can be helpful.

*Examples of alternative credit can be child care, insurances, electric and cell bills or even "buy-here-pay-here" retailers. Because you are paying these items on a reoccurring basis, they count as normal credit if reported to the bureaus. You will need to specifically request that the credit bureau request information from those companies. Chances are that you have been paying these alternative payments for a while and will, thus, add age to your file. There is information in the appendix regarding contact information for each of the credit bureaus.

Newly active borrowers will see optimum results in 12 – 24 month, so patience must become your new best friend.

Key #4
New Credit
10%

Definition: How recently a new credit item was opened

Every time a new account is reported to the credit bureau, the credit score is reduced. However, the reduction is typically for a short time such as six months. New accounts are necessary, but opening many new ones can really damage your score, so be mindful of the consequences of each new account you open. Here is some more information about this subject.

- Any new credit will hurt a credit score for a time, even if one's credit profile is long-established.

- Lots of new accounts will be very detrimental to a score.

- Typically, credit scores recover in approximately 6 – 12 months.

- Newly acquired credit may be necessary for long term improvement. Over time, new credit cards may be favorable to spread out credit balances. New accounts will not be as detrimental to a credit score as a high outstanding to maximum balance ratio as discussed in Key #2.

- No new account is opened without that new lender reviewing your credit report. Every time your credit is reviewed, a "Credit Inquiry" is registered on your report. These inquiries will also reduce your scores, even if no new credit is established! Thus, always examine the benefits vs. the consequences when considering those "on the spot" discounts for opening a new account—it may cause more harm than the discount is worth.

Seasoned credit is the ideal model.
New credit may be necessary and beneficial in long run.

Key #5
Types of Credit
10%

Definition: Installment vs. Revolving

No, all credit accounts are not created equally. The harder it is to get a credit account, the more heavily it is weighted in the credit score. Thus, a home loan (Installment) is weighted much more heavily than a department store card (revolving).

- Credit accounts with periodic, level payments have the most positive impact on scores, i.e. auto or mortgage (installment).

- Credit accounts with varying, open-ended terms are the least positive to score determination, i.e., credit cards, finance companies, and "buy-her-pay-here accounts (Revolving).

- Credit accounts with varying, open-ended terms are usually at higher interest rates and are, thus, considered to become more difficult to pay.

- Each type of new credit affects your score differently—auto loans paid as agreed will have a stronger positive impact on scores than do credit cards.

- If all reported credit is revolving (credit cards), obtaining installment debt (auto/mortgage) will increase scores over time.

Maintain a level mix of accounts.

How Long is a Credit Score Impacted?

Bankruptcy	7-10 years
Late Payments	7 years
Collections	7 years
Judgments	7 years
Foreclosures	2-5 years
Short Sales	2-5 years
Tax Liens	Indefinite
Credit Inquiries	2 years

The more time away from an event, the lesser the score impact. A credit score will improve gradually over the above mentioned timelines, however, the event will cause some impact for the entire period.

Historical Data Proves Accurate

- *Those with credit scores under 580 are*
  62%
  more likely to perform poorly.

- *Those with credit scores under 620 are*
  27%
  more likely to perform poorly.

- *Those with credit scores over 700 are*
  < 3%
  likely to perform poorly.

The Five Keys

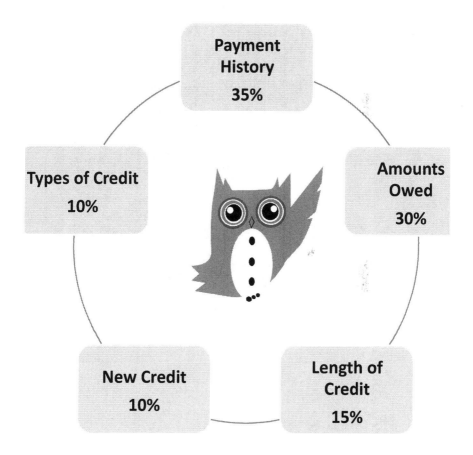

WIZE Thoughts

There are Five Key Components in the credit score calculation

The Numbers have proven to accurately predict future behavior.

Lenders rely on Credit Scores.

CHAPTER 7

Let's Get To Work!

Manage My Credit
...How do You begin?

An action plan is your first step.

1. Order a copy of your credit report.

2. Read all of the information included.

3. If errors are found, contact the bureaus immediately.

4. Identify areas for improvement.

5. Subscribe to a credit monitoring service.

Now, Let's discuss each step...

#1 Order a Copy of Your Credit Report

Options:

- Order directly from each of the three bureaus*

- Order from a free online source*

- Subscribe for identity theft, and request report*

- Always be protective of your personal information

necessary contact information is in the appendix

#2 Read All of the Information Included on your report

- Check for accuracy

    (Spelling, birth date, addresses)

- Many credit reports contain substantial errors

    (Inaccurate reporting of payment history is most common)

- Ask for clarity if confusing

    (Any banker can help, all three bureaus will assist)

- Do not share report with others.

    (Remember that the report contains your complete financial fingerprint)

#3 If Errors are Found,
Contact the Bureaus Immediately

- Contact all three bureaus to dispute errors*

    (Experian, Equifax, Transunion – all have forms to complete and toll-free numbers to call)

- Contact specific creditors to correct error

    (Contact information for creditors is included in the report)

- Create and maintain your own records

    (You must provide evidence to reverse the error)

- Maintain communication with bureaus and creditor until error is corrected

    (Keep records of all conversations, contacts, and dates of communication)

- Never give up

    (Remember, it is your property to maintain)

- Errors must be corrected if they are truly errors

    (Laws protect you)

*contact information in appendix

#4 Identify Areas of Improvement

- Check your information against the Five Keys

    (history, balances, types, new accounts, and length of profile)

- Pay any currently late payments immediately

    (Most impactful – 35% of score determination)

- Redistribute credit card exposure

    (30% outstanding debt vs maximum available)

- Consider moving revolving debt to installment

    (Personal loan, Line of credit against home)

- Check inquiries for any unauthorized by you

    (Existing creditors may access report without renewed authorization)

#5 Subscribe to a Credit Monitoring Service

- Credit monitoring service notifies you of all activity on your report

- Notifications are sent when new activity takes place for your verification

- New activity by anyone other than you can be stopped immediately

- Helps to protect your identity

- Full credit reports are available for viewing through these services

- Available from many sources, such as, Costco, AMEX, banks, credit unions, credit cards, etc.*

- Monthly fees are usually charged—$10 - $25 is typical

*See appendix

WIZE Thoughts

Start by obtaining, reading and understanding your credit report.

Develop a plan of action that you can handle.

Protect yourself.

CHAPTER 8

What are the
Next Steps?

Now that you have your Credit Profile in hand,
let's look at what you can do
to create the credit profile of your dreams.

Let's first discuss establishing a

New Credit Profile.

If you are just starting out or if your credit has been dormant for years, here are some great ways to begin...

You Could...

Obtain a Secured Loan,
also called a
"Savings Account Loan"

Most banks will issue an installment loan using a savings account as collateral. If you open a $300 savings account, they may give you a loan for $300 and will hold your savings account as collateral. This type of loan shows on your credit report as a "Paid as Agreed" loan over the term of the loan. Once it is paid off, request a new loan, maybe for $500, and then continue in this manner.

Although you relinquish use of the money in the savings account during the term of the loan, it may earn interest and launch your healthy credit profile.

OR...you could...

Obtain a Credit Card with a Small Credit Limit

- Most banks and many credit card companies will issue a credit card to a new user with a very low maximum available loan limit such as $500.

- Usually, obtaining a new credit card through your bank or credit union will carry a better interest rate than one offered by a mail solicitation.

- The best way to start a healthy credit file using a credit card is to charge only an amount that can be paid down to a zero balance monthly.

- It is critical that the card is never used to charge items up to the maximum limit, and then only to make just minimum payments. That is a huge mistake and really negates all benefit from obtaining the account.

- If a new credit card is obtained, use it, but sparingly. Use it; pay it off; repeat.

OR...you could...

Obtain Credit Utilizing a Cosigner

- This method of credit creation is a good one if, and only if, all parties are fully aware of the consequences.

- First, what is a cosigner? A cosigner is typically a relative who allows the lender to review their income, assets, and credit in the hopes of strengthening a new borrower's loan application.

- However, a cosigner's good credit does not overcome the original applicant's bad credit, only their lack of it.

- If a cosigner is used, they are EQUALLY liable for the debt, and any credit reporting (including late pays) will be added to their credit report. Thus, it is crucial that all parties understand that if a payment is late, BOTH parties will be damaged.

So be sure that BOTH Grandpa and Jr. understand the rules.

OR...you could...

Request non-traditional debts be placed on your report

- Often people have created credit but are not aware that it is useable on a credit report because it is not from a bank or other traditional lender. However, credit can be created from any repetitious, periodic payments made.

- For instance, most cell phone companies do not report to the credit bureaus; however, if you do not make the monthly payment, you will no longer have that cell service, right? Thus, you have created credit! Also, monthly bills for utilities, home telephone, cable, and childcare can be considered a form of credit.

- Although these types of credit may not be as heavily weighted as, say, a bank-issued auto loan, they can get you started. You must contact the bureaus* and the companies to request they be placed onto your credit profile.

- Typically, a new lender will want to see at least four companies reporting a 24-month pattern to have an established profile. Regardless of what you have, it is a start.

P.S. If you have NOT paid any of these companies on time….do not request that they be reported!

* See appendix for contact information.

Now that you have started...

How long will it take to have the new accounts sufficiently established to provide an accurate credit score?

- Lenders agree that one or two new lines of credit do not sufficiently represent an established payment history.

- Typically, a lender will want to see four credit entries that have been opened for 12 – 24 months before they are confident they see an accurate picture of how you handle your obligations.

- Later, you will see how long it takes for derogatory credit to disappear from your report....as you can guess, one neglected account can damage you for a long time.

Remember... *Start slowly and stay in control!*

Now let's discuss repairing past damaged credit...

Hey, life happens, right? Fortunately, getting back on track is not as overwhelming as it may seem. The step-by-step process will take some time, however, the feeling of accomplishment you will have with each improvement will make it all worthwhile!

Your next steps:

- Pay any past due payments to a current status....MOST IMPORTANT, remember payment history is the most heavily weighted portion of your credit score.

- Rebalance outstanding credit.

- Introduce installment credit to your profile.

- Obtain new credit.

- Consider other methods (such as bankruptcy).

Bring Any Past Due Payments
to a
Current Status.

- This is the most important step toward improving your credit score

- Payment history = 35% of your credit score calculation

- You may need to budget JUST to catch up

   1.   Make a list of past-due payments, lowest to highest

   2.   Determine what you can pay the fastest

   3.   Determine step 2, 3, etc., while staying current on those just paid

   4.   Write payment plan and review daily or weekly until all past-dues are current

   5.   Once all are current, continue all currently required payments

   6.   Move to step 2 in your overall plan

- Call any creditors to whom you owe past due amounts*

- Creditors will often arrange a payment plan that will work for you

- Creditors will often remove old, derogatory credit report information if current for over two years

- A huge part of credit correction is communicating with creditors

*creditor contact information is usually listed within your credit report

Rebalance Outstanding Credit

- This is the 2nd most heavily weighted portion of your credit score (30%)

- Remember, the ideal credit model is to have outstanding balances equal to no more than 30% of available credit

  Example:
  - Maximum available credit level $3000

  - Optimal outstanding   x 30%

  - Ideal outstanding credit = $0.00 - $900.00 will keep you under the magic 30% level.

- If paying down an outstanding balance quickly is not possible, ask credit card companies to increase your available credit limits. Your ratio will go down automatically, but <u>do not charge more to your account!!!</u>

- Although it seems counterintuitive, it is better to have multiple credit accounts with low balances than one account with a high current balance to available credit ratio

  Why?
- The higher the balance to available credit ratio, the more the credit scoring engine thinks you are using all credit available rather than being cautious in your credit usage. The more outstanding AVAILABLE but UNUSED credit you have the better.

- Additionally, many credit cards will offer very low interest rates on Balance Transfers. If you choose this route, focus on paying the balance down/off during the low interest period.

Going forward, Best Practice:
Pay down balances to 30% of available credit amount
Redistribute outstanding debt over a number of credit sources

Introduce Installment Credit
to Your Profile

- The type of credit you have impacts 15% of your credit score

- An installment loan has equal payments over a set period of time such as an auto or home loan

- Revolving credit has varying payment over an unlimited period of time and is of less value to your score than installment. Credit cards are an example of revolving credit accounts

- An installment loan (auto or mortgage) carries more positive weight to your score

- *If neither an auto nor home loan are possible, request an installment loan secured by a* deposit account as was discussed under the "Establishing New Credit" section.

Obtain New Credit
Although this sounds contrary to the message, it may be a good choice

- *A strong credit profile contains at least four credit items active for a minimum of 24 months. If you have only one or two items, a new account will help over time.*

- *New credit <u>must</u> be used sparingly and in a controlled manner.*

- *New credit along with the associated inquiries will decrease your credit scores in the short term, but will strengthen them over time.*

- You can also reactivate old credit. Those accounts will appear to be seasoned ones.

Other possible paths you may consider...

Bankruptcy: A legal proceeding involving a person or business that is unable to repay outstanding debts.

- Debts named in the bankruptcy (BK) will be forgiven and are no longer the responsibility of the borrower

- Not all debts MAY be named in a BK. For instance, most student loans and tax liens may not be included

- Not all debts MUST be included in a BK, for instance, an auto loan and a mortgage may be excluded

- The courts will decide if a BK will be awarded after review of all debts and assets

- It is critical that remaining and new credit is paid as agreed following a BK

- Poor credit history after the BK is awarded ("a clean slate") is very unfavorable to a new creditor

- A BK is very damaging to one's credit score and will have impact for up to 10 years*

*However, many lenders will consider issuing new credit 2-3 years following the full settlement of the BK. But, a higher than normal interest rate may be charged.

Credit Counseling: Services that assist in negotiating, restructuring and bundling debt for the purpose of easing the payment burden and avoiding bankruptcy.

- Counseling companies may charge a fee; however, there are also not-for-profit agencies as well

- Typically the companies cannot eliminate debt, but rearrange the payment into a more manageable plan, often combining all payments into one. The new payment should be less than your current monthly out of pocket

- Typically, plans will take 2 – 10 years to complete the payoff of your debts

- Accounts included in credit counseling will typically be identified on your credit report and will negatively affect your credit score until the plan is completed

- Typically, while in credit counseling, new installment credit (auto or home) is very difficult to obtain

Dispute Inaccurate Information: Formally disagreeing with reported information.*

- If you find errors on your credit report, it is up to you to dispute the information. You must also provide correct information, supported with documentation if possible

- If you dispute an account, the credit bureaus will research and correct IF the lender agrees that there is an error

- Lenders typically have 30 days to respond. However, as always, it is up to you to follow up with both the lender and with the credit bureaus

- When an account is stated to be a "Disputed Account" on your credit report, any information regarding that account is not used in the credit score calculation. It is as if it does not exist

- **HOWEVER,** if a new lender sees a "Disputed Account", it may not issue you a new loan because the disputed account has an unknown outcome, and the credit score is not a true representation of your credit profile. Your new loan may be delayed until the dispute is settled

- Before you dispute any account, have written documentation that proves the error if possible

Again, it is up to you!

*Sample letters are included in appendix.

Now, Let's Discuss Taking Your Good Credit to Great Credit.

You may be thinking, "If I have good a credit score, why should I care about all of this?"

Well, moving your credit score from good to GREAT can make a big difference in the interest rate you may pay.

Remember, the higher the credit score, the lower the interest rate.

With a GREAT credit score, you could save thousands of dollars over the life of a loan.

Make a Habit of Reviewing
Your Credit Report on a
Regular Basis

- For those of you who have a long-established, healthy credit profile, you are our heroes! Even if you have a perfect credit score—no one does, by the way!—it is still critically important that you protect your valuable and hard-earned property. You, too, must monitor your credit on a regular basis. Because you are a strong credit candidate, you may be an even more appealing target for identity theft, so it may be even more important for you to stay aware.

- There are many options you may use to obtain your credit report on a regular basis.

- Companies that provide Identity Theft Protection (ITP) are plentiful and relatively inexpensive. If you do subscribe to an ITP plan, you will be notified whenever there is any activity under your social security number. If you did not create the action, you can stop any further unlawful use of your information immediately.

- Additionally, you can freeze your credit profile completely so that no activity can take place prior to your unlocking the file. More on that later.

Protecting your precious property is your job,
so never assume that you can be on autopilot!

AND...

Review
for
Errors

- *Alarmingly, the majority of all credit reports contain errors. If you have long-established credit, you are a perfect candidate for errors because so much data has been reported over the years. When you have a copy of your report, simply look for any derogatory comments with which you disagree (and can prove it).*

- *Additionally, check for current balances that are off by more than a few months' payments. Often that last payment does not get reported to the bureaus. A phone call to the creditor can clear that up within a few days.*

- *Any paid public records that have been filed against you may still be showing as outstanding. Here is where keeping your records is essential to a speedy correction. Contact the bureaus and provide your evidence to justify the correction. They are required to validate and correct or tell you why they cannot.*

Again, your credit is your possession to which you must show continual attention for optimum performance.

AND...

Redistribute Debt
to
Improve Score

One of the biggest reasons for a less-than-perfect credit score is a misdistribution of debt. If you have a good credit rating, you may be able to move to the stratosphere of a GREAT score with a redistribution of your debt load. Remember, one of the Five Keys that effects credit is to have no more than 30% outstanding balance against the maximum credit allowed. Thus, it may be beneficial to move some debt from one high-balance credit account to another with a low existing balance.

Remember, it is a fallacy that having one credit card is better than having five. If that high balance is distributed to five low-balance cards, your credit score will improve. Although the dollar amount may be exactly the same, it appears that you now have much more credit available to you that you are not using—you are in control of your spending habits. Whereas, if you have one card that is maxed out, it appears that you are using all the credit available to you.

A zero-balance card does very little to affect your score; however, well-distributed debt carries the second most heavily weighted factor in score calculation.

AND...

Never
Become
Complacent

Identity theft is growing quickly all over the world. Chances are good that either you or someone you know has been a victim. It could have been as minor as someone capturing your debit card information at a restaurant, or as catastrophic as someone hacking your banking information.

Either way, one case of theft can lead to one's entire identity being used by someone else. Without keeping a close eye on your precious possession—your hard-earned good credit—it can be gone in a few weeks. That is why you must stay vigilant.

There are many tools available to keep you connected.
Some are in the appendix of this book. Many more are out there...

Find them, use them!

Finally, let's discuss
a few universal steps
that apply to *everyone*,
regardless of their credit condition.

1. Keep your records.

2. Dispute inaccurate information

3. Be patient

4. Be even more patient.

#1 Keep Your Records

It is important to think of your credit as your property and responsibility. It is not the responsibility of the credit bureaus to report accurate histories but only information sent to them by your creditors. It is incumbent upon your creditors to report your payment history accurately; however, data can be entered incorrectly or not in a timely manner. Thus, it is up to you to keep your own accurate records.

If you do have credit items that require any correspondence, you must keep copies of anything exchanged between you and the creditor. Thus, if you do see that there are inaccuracies on your report, you can justify your challenge. Also, keep copies of cancelled checks or money order receipts. Any verification of registered mail and validation of receipt can also be invaluable. Banks and credit unions will have all cancelled checks and other transaction instruments as digital record. Never be afraid to ask for their help.

Maneuvering through the maze of legal records and postings can be overwhelming. If you keep your records, you can provide information to the bureaus. They will then have a path to follow for corrections. If not, the time it may take to get erroneous items removed or updated can be extreme.

Think of your credit the same as you would your home or car.
If you want them to be cared for, it is up to you.

Your credit is no different.

#2 Dispute Inaccurate Information
(this section bears repeating!)

- If you find errors on your credit report, it is up to you to dispute the information. You must also provide correct information supported with documentation if possible.

- If you dispute an account, the credit bureaus will research and correct IF the lender agrees there is an error.

- Lenders typically have 30 days to respond. However, as always, it is up to you follow up with both the lender and the credit bureau.

- When an account is stated to be a "Disputed Account" on your credit report, any information regarding that account is not used in the credit score calculation. It is as if it does not exist.

- HOWEVER, if a new lender sees a Disputed Account, they may not issue you a new loan because the disputed account has an unknown outcome, and the credit score is not a true representation of your credit profile. Your new loan may be delayed until the dispute is settled.

- Before you dispute any account, have written documentation that proves the error if possible.

Again, it is up to you.

#3 Be Patient

Any changes or improvements will take time.

Below are the approximate timeframes.

- Corrected credit should take approximately 60 days to appear

- Corrected public records may take 120 days to appear

- New credit should take approximately 60 days to appear

- Any credit changes can appear at any time during a month

- Full benefit to new credit will take 12 – 24 months

- Credit disputes can take 6 months or more to resolve*

- A strong credit model will have a minimum of four accounts with perfect payment history for a minimum of 24 months

* Keep all paperwork of credit issues. Providing that information to the bureaus can speed up the correction process.

#4 Be even more Patient!

Reported negative activity may remain on your report as follows:

- Tax Liens ....Indefinite

- Bankruptcy ....7 – 10 years

- Late Payments ....7 years

- Collections ....7 years

- Judgments ....7 years

- Foreclosure ....2 – 5 years

- Short Sale...2 -5 years

- Credit Inquiries ....2 years

However, that the more time that passes from the event, the less the impact on your score. There will always be some impact for the terms stated, but the reduction in score will less and less over time.

WIZE Thoughts

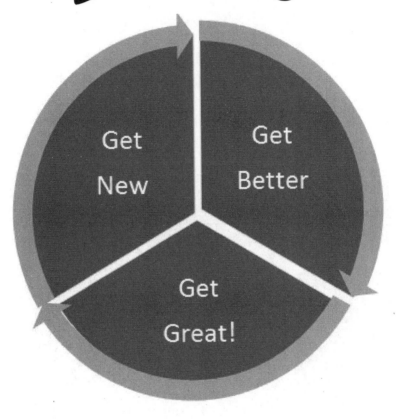

Get New

Get Better

Get Great!

CHAPTER 9

Public Records

Public Records:
Legal Recordings of Tax Liens, Lawsuits, Collections, and Judgments

- Legal recordings appear in the county in which the action occurred.

- Because these recordings are available to the public, no Social Security numbers are used, only names and addresses.

- Public records are *not automatically* reported to the credit bureaus.

- Often, public records are MANUALLY retrieved and reported to the bureaus by individuals employed by the bureaus.

- Because recordings are researched by name and address, mistakes are common.

- Smaller counties often contained public records that are never discovered.

More

about

Public Records...

- Collections, judgments, and tax liens result from non-payment of an obligation.

- The creditor appeals to the courts for legal action to collection of the debt.

- Creditors must notify all parties prior to appealing to the courts for legal action.

- Most states require a 30-day notice.

- Creditors will mail one or more notices to the last known address of the borrower.

- Collection of the debt may result in simple recordation of the debt with the hope of future payment.

- Collection of the debt may also result in garnishment of wages, retention of tax refunds, or liens against property*.

- Once filed, a public record will remain on your credit report for 3 – 10 years.

*If a debt is recorded as a lien against a property, it must be paid in the event the property is sold or refinanced.

Public Records...
What to do....

- Never ignore notice of legal action. Call the lender directly to work out a plan.

- Most creditors will accept minimal payments if action is taken early in the process.

- Many creditors will negotiate a lower payoff if action is taken early in the process.

- Any partial payment or negotiated payoff is much more difficult once a debt is turned over to a collection agency.

- Once a debt is paid in full—even a negotiated amount—a Satisfaction (pay off) of Debt is recorded.

Public Records...

Your Actions

- As with any debt, it is *your responsibility* to follow up on the recordation of the pay off AND that the credit bureaus are aware of the recordation of the satisfaction.

- Remember, the bureaus may have no way to know if a satisfaction has been recorded if you do not tell them.

- Keep your records of all correspondence, conversations, and contacts throughout the process....

It is up to YOU to set the record straight.

Public Records
...the Odd Thing

Avoiding having public records is always the best way to go. However, if a public record is filed, your credit score will be greatly impacted.

HOWEVER, as with any negative event on a credit report, the further away from the occurrence, the less impact on your credit score. That is GOOD NEWS, right? _Well maybe_. As odd as it may seem, paying an old public record may actually hurt your credit score AGAIN! The credit-scoring machine sees only that something new has happened, not _what_ has happened. However, the negative hit is fairly short-lived as the scoring engine now reads the outstanding balance as zero.

The lesson learned here is, first, <u>negotiate</u> early in the process so there is no public record in the first place.

But, it you are faced with the situation and want to purchase a home or other major item, discuss payment of the recorded debt with your lender before you actually apply. They may help you with when and how to pay the debt that will be the best for your credit score in the long run.

New guidelines are proposed to be enacted in 2015 that will lessen the impact of medical collections on credit scores. Additionally, once any collection is paid to a zero balance —and reported as such—the "odd thing" we discussed earlier is said to be reduced. At this writing, the new guidelines are still proposed only.

WIZE Thoughts

Do Not Ignore Notices

Negotiate early in the process

Your Job is to insure accurate recordings

CHAPTER 10

What About Credit Monitoring?

Protect Your Identity
Every 4 Seconds,

Someone is the Victim of Identity Theft.*

How Identity Thieves Operate

Dumpster diving – *searching for items containing your personal information*

Skimming – *stealing credit/debit card number by using a specialized storage device when you use your card*

Phishing – *pretending to be financial institutions or companies via email requesting your personal information*

Changing your address – *diverting your billing statements to another simply by completing a change of address form*

Stealing – *simply stealing your wallet, purses, or mailbox*

Pretexting – *using false pretenses to obtain your personal information from banks, cell companies, etc.*

Cloning – *recreating your debit card for use*

*www.idtheftcenter.org

Monitoring your credit…

it's a MUST!!!

- Many companies provide credit-monitoring services*

- Banks, credit card companies, big retail stores will offer

- Most will charge monthly fees; $15 - $35 is normal

- You will be contacted when any new activity occurs

*See appendix

Freezing...
Another Option

- Freezing your entire credit profile will require your approval PRIOR to any new activity

- Freezing your entire credit profile is requested from the three bureaus directly*

- There may be a minimal fee charged to freeze your account with each bureau

- Your credit profiles can be activated by you only via your personal pass code

- Your credit profile can be active only after you have "unlocked" it, including activity you may initiate

* See appendix

Steps to take if you are a victim of identity theft

- Notify all three credit bureaus*

- Notify all creditors that have been affected

- Notify the Federal Trade Commission hotline*

- Notify local police to file theft report

- Keep copies of all correspondence, names, and dates

- Take charge, it is your responsibility, not that of the credit bureau

- Don't give up!

*See appendix

Monitor,
Monitor,
Monitor

Remember that your credit is your property, and just like any other item that you own, checking in on its condition is crucial to maintaining its good condition. Thus, you must start with simply getting a copy of your credit report*. Without that, you will not know what you are dealing with.

Once you have examined your report, you can determine if there are errors as well as formulate a plan to strengthen your credit profile.

You must then stay on a review schedule. It could be monthly, quarterly, or annually. Whatever you choose, choose something. There are many suggestions for credit monitoring in the appendix of this book. There are many other options as well.

The main thing is to make a commitment to yourself to get and keep your credit profile as accurate as possible. It is up to you.

*See Appendix

WIZE Thoughts

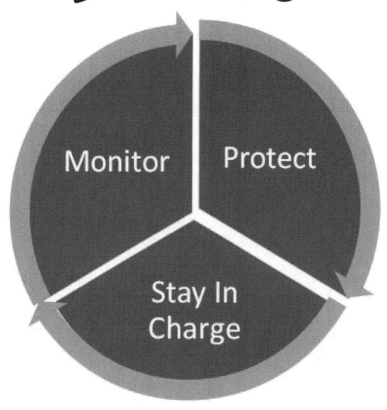

Summary

Credit creation, repair, and maintenance is a lifelong process that requires knowledge, dedication, and commitment. Credit should not be mysterious nor intimidating. Credit should serve you to have the best life possible.

We sincerely hope that this information is a valuable tool in helping you to look boldly to the future with the confidence and power that only you can create.

Appendix

Definitions

Annual Fee

Credit card issuers often (but not always) require you to pay a special charge once a year for the use of their service, usually between $15 and $55.

Annual Percentage Rate (APR)

A measure of how much interest credit will cost you, expressed as an annual percentage.

Authorized User

Person permitted by a credit cardholder to charge goods and services on the cardholder's account but who is not responsible for the debt. The account displays on the credit reports of the cardholder as well as the authorized user. If you wish to have your name permanently removed as an authorized user on an account, you will need to notify the credit grantor.

Balloon Payments

A loan with a balloon payment requires that a single, lump-sum payment be made at the end of the loan.

Bankruptcy - Chapter 7

Bankruptcy chapter of the Bankruptcy Code that provides for court administered liquidation of the assets of a financially troubled individual or business.

Bankruptcy – Chapter 11

Bankruptcy chapter of the Bankruptcy Code that is usually used for the reorganization of a financially troubled business. Used as an alternative to liquidation under Chapter 7. The US Supreme Court has held that an individual may also use Chapter 11.

Bankruptcy – Chapter 12

Bankruptcy chapter of the Bankruptcy Code adopted to address the financial crisis of the nation's farming community. Cases under this chapter are administered like Chapter 11 cases, but with special protections to meet the special conditions of family farm operations.

Bankruptcy – Chapter 13

Bankruptcy chapter of the Bankruptcy Code in which debtors repay debts according to a plan accepted by the debtor, the creditors, and the court. Plan payments usually come from the debtor's future income and are paid to creditors through the court system and the bankruptcy trustee.

Charge-Off

Action of transferring accounts deemed uncollectible to a category such as bad debt or loss. Collectors will usually continue to solicit payments, but the accounts are no longer considered part of a company's receivable or profit picture.

Closed Ended

A debt with a maximum loan amount established at the start of the loan, such as a mortgage.

Collection

Recorded document reserving the right to collect a debt at a future date.

Cosigner

Person who pledges in writing as part of a credit contract to repay the debt if the borrower fails to do so. The account displays on both the borrower's and the cosigner's credit reports.

Credit Limit/Line of Credit

In open-end credit, the maximum amount a borrower can draw upon or the maximum that an account can show as outstanding.

Credit Items

Information reported by current or past creditors.

Credit Report

Confidential report on a consumer's payment habits as reported by their creditors to a consumer credit reporting agency. The agency provides the information to credit grantors who have a permissible purpose under the law to review the report.

Credit Scoring

Tool used by credit agencies to provide an objective means of determining risks in granting credit. Credit scoring increases efficiency and timely response in the credit granting process. Credit scoring criteria is set by the credit agency.

Date Filed

The date that a public record was awarded.

Date of Status

On the credit report, date the creditor last reported information about the account.

Date Opened

On the credit report, indicates the date an account was opened.

Date Resolved

The completion date or satisfaction date of a public record item.

Delinquent Accounts

Credit items classified into categories according to the time past due. Common classifications are 30, 60, 90, and 120 days past due. Special classifications also include charge-off, repossession, transferred, etc.

Discharge Granted

Issued by the court to release a debtor from most of his debts that were included in a bankruptcy. Any debts not included in the bankruptcy—alimony, child support, liability for willful and malicious conduct, and certain student loans—cannot be discharged.

Dismissed

When a consumer files a bankruptcy, the judge may decide to not allow the consumer to continue with the bankruptcy. If the judge rules against the petition, the bankruptcy is known as dismissed.

Dispute

If a consumer believes an item of information on their credit report is inaccurate or incomplete, they may challenge or dispute the item. Credit agencies will investigate and correct or remove any inaccurate information or information that cannot be verified.

Finance Charge

Amount of interest. Finance charges are usually included in the monthly payment total.

Fixed Rate

An annual percentage rate that does not change.

Foreclosure

A procedure that permits a lender, in the event of a loan default, to have the mortgaged property sold in order to cover some or all of the remaining debt.

Grace Period

The time period you have to pay a bill in full and avoid interest and/or late payment penalty charges.

Guarantor

Person responsible for paying a debt if the original borrower fails to pay, also known as a co-signor.

Installment Credit

Credit account in which the debt is divided into amounts to be paid successively at specified intervals.

Judgment

A court order to the loser of a lawsuit to pay the winner a specified sum of money.

Involuntary Bankruptcy

A petition filed by certain credit grantors to have a debtor judged bankrupt. If the bankruptcy is granted, it is known as an involuntary bankruptcy.

Liability Amount

Amount for which you are legally obligated to a creditor.

Lien

Legal document used to create a security interest in another's property. A lien can be placed against a consumer for failure to pay the city, county, state, or federal government money that is owed. It means that the consumer's property is being used as collateral during repayment of the money that is owed.

Line of Credit

In open-end credit, the maximum amount a borrower can draw upon or the maximum that an account can show as outstanding.

Location Number

The book and page number on which the item is filed in the court records.

Obsolescence

A term used to describe how long negative information should stay in a credit file before it is no longer relevant to the credit granting decision. For example, the obsolescence period for a bankruptcy is 10 years. Unpaid tax liens may remain indefinitely.

Open Ended

A debt for which the maximum allowable loan amount can vary throughout the period of the debt, such as on a credit card.

Opt In

The ability of a consumer who has opted out to have their name re-added to prescreened credit and insurance offer lists, direct marketing lists, and individual reference service lists. Consumers who have previously opted out of receiving prescreened offers may have their names added to prescreened lists for credit and insurance offers by calling 1-888-567-8688.

Opt Out

The ability of the consumer to notify credit reporting agencies, direct marketers, and list compliers to remove their name from all future lists. Consumers may opt out of prescreened credit and insurance offer lists by calling 1-888-567-8688.

Permissible Purposes

There are legally defined permissible purposes for a credit report to be issued to third party. Permissible purposes included credit transactions, employment purposes, insurance underwriting, government financial responsibility laws, court orders, subpoenas, written instructions of the consumer, legitimate business needs, etc.

Petition

If a consumer files a bankruptcy, but a judge has not yet ruled that it can proceed, it is known as a bankruptcy petitioned.

Plaintiff

One who initially brings legal action against another (defendant) seeking a court decision.

Public Record Data

Included as part of the credit report, this information is limited to tax liens, lawsuits, and judgments that relate to the consumer's debt obligations.

Released

This means that a lien has been satisfied in full.

Repossession

A creditor's taking possession of property pledged as collateral on a loan contract for which a borrower has fallen significantly behind in payments.

Request an Investigation

If you believe that information on your credit report is inaccurate, the credit agency will ask the sources of the information to check their records at no cost to you. Incorrect information will be corrected, and information that cannot be verified will be deleted. A credit bureau cannot remove accurate information nor any information without verified information from the creditor.

Revolving Account

Credit automatically available to a predetermined maximum limit so long as a customer makes regular payments.

Risk Scoring Models

A numerical determination of a consumer's creditworthiness. A tool used by credit grantors to predict future payment behavior of a consumer based on past performance.

Satisfied

If the consumer has paid all of the money the court says he owes, the public record item is satisfied.

Secured Credit

Loan for which some form of acceptable collateral, such as a house or automobile, has been pledged.

Security

Real or personal property that a borrower pledges for the term of the loan. Should the borrower fail to repay, the creditor may take ownership of the property by following legally mandated procedures.

Short Sale

An agreed upon sale price of property that is less than the mortgage balance. Both the individual owner and the lender must agree on the amount.

Terms

This refers to the debt repayment terms of your agreement with a creditor, such as 60 months, 48 months, etc.

Third-Party Collectors

Collectors who are under contract to collect debts for a credit department or credit company and work for a collection company.

Truth in Lending Act

Title I of the Consumer Protection Act. Requires that most categories of lenders disclose the annual interest rate, the total dollar cost, and other terms of loans and credit sales.

Vacated

Indicates a judgment that was rendered void or set aside

Variable Rate

An annual percentage rate that may change over time as the prime lending rate varies or according to your contract with the lender

Victim Statement

A statement that can be added to a consumer's credit report to alert credit grantors that a consumer's identification has been used fraudulently to obtain credit. The statement requests the credit grantor to contact the consumer by telephone before issuing credit. It remains on file for 7 years unless the consumer requests that it be removed.

Voluntary Bankruptcy

If a consumer files the bankruptcy on his own, it is known as voluntary bankruptcy.

Wage Garnishment

The collection of a debt via one's wages received directly from the employer.

Withdrawn

The decision was made to not pursue a bankruptcy, a lien, etc., after court document have been filed.

Writ of Replevin

Legal document issued by a court authorizing repossession of security.

RESOURCES

All resources included herein are for reference only. The author has no affiliation nor does she endorse any specific referral source listed.

Annual Amortization Table
$100,000 Loan Amount,
4.5% Interest

Monthly Payment	Total of 360 Payments	Total Interest Paid	Payoff Date
$506.69	$182,406.71	$82,406.71	May. 12, 2044

Amortization Table
⦿ Annual ◯ Monthly

Date	Principal	Interest	Balance
2014	$932.23	$2,614.56	$99,067.77
2015	$2,588.29	$7,038.74	$97,411.71
2016	$4,320.42	$11,386.83	$95,679.58
2017	$6,132.12	$15,655.34	$93,867.88
2018	$8,027.06	$19,840.63	$91,972.94
2019	$10,009.05	$23,938.87	$89,990.95
2020	$12,082.09	$27,946.05	$87,917.91
2021	$14,250.36	$31,858.00	$85,749.64
2022	$16,518.25	$35,670.34	$83,481.75
2023	$18,890.32	$39,378.49	$81,109.68
2024	$21,371.37	$42,977.67	$78,628.63
2025	$23,966.39	$46,462.9_	$76,033.61
2026	$26,680.63	$49,828._	$73,319.37
2027	$29,519.56	$5_,070.1_	$70,480.44
2028	$32,488.9_	$56,_81.02	$67,511.09
2029	$35,5_.67	$59,155.48	$64,405.33
2030	$38,8_.1_	$61,987.27	$61,156.89
2031	$42,240.78	$64,669.82	$57,759.22
2032	$45,794.54	$67,196.28	$54,205.46
2033	$49,511.56	$69,559.48	$50,488.44
2034	$53,399.34	$71,751.93	$46,600.66
2035	$57,465.73	$73,765.77	$42,534.27
2036	$61,718.92	$75,592.80	$38,281.08
2037	$66,167.50	$77,224.44	$33,832.50
2038	$70,820.45	$78,651.72	$29,179.55
2039	$75,687.16	$79,865.23	$24,312.84
2040	$80,777.44	$80,855.18	$19,222.56
2041	$86,101.57	$81,611.27	$13,898.43
2042	$91,670.28	$82,122.78	$8,329.72
2043	$97,494.83	$82,378.46	$2,505.17
2044	$100,000.00	$82,406.71	$0.00

CREDIT BUREAUS

Experian

P.O. box 2104
Allen, Texas 75132
(888) Experian
(397-3742)
www.experian/help.com

Equifax

P.O. box 740241
Atlanta, Georgia 30374
(800) 685-1111
www.equifax.com\FCRA

Transunion

P.O. box 2000
Chester, Pennsylvania 29011
(800) 680-7289
www.transunion.com

CREDIT REPORTS

- Annualcreditreport.com
- Freescoreonline.com
- Experian.com
- Creditkarma.com

CREDIT CARD SOURCE

- Comparecards.com
- Americanexpress.com/creditsource
- Local banks and credit unions

STUDENT LOAN ASSISTANCE

Studentdebtrelief.us
1-866-921-8053

NationalSLC.com
1-888-644-3512

Studentloanreliefgroup.com
1888-659-6532

Staffordloan.com
1-800-4FED-AID

Your Personal Banker

FINANCIAL COUNSELORS

- Moneymangement.org
- Familyfoundations.org
- AdvantageCCS.org
- Christaincredit@ibudget.org
- Ibudget.org
- nfcc.org/firststep
(National Foundation for Credit Counseling)

CREDIT MONITORING

- American Express
- TrustedID.com
- Lifelock.com
- Identityguard.com
- Your local bank may offer the service as well.
- Many other options

Sample #1:
Credit Correction Letter

Dear Credit Bureau,

After receiving a copy of my credit report and checking my records, I have found incorrect information. My name is John Doe, and I reside at 2233 Park Avenue, Any Town, California 22222. My social security number is 111-22-3333. My previous address was 6143 Summer Lane, Any Town, California 22222. My birthdate is 11-17-50.

I do not have an account with Brewer's Collection, account #12456.

My account at Nelson's Department Store, #4441, was paid in full as agreed and should have a positive rating.

This bankruptcy, docket #45667, for $100,000, 10-12-88, is wrong and should not be on my report. This is not mine.

Sincerely,
John Doe

Sample #2:
Credit Correction Letter

Dear Credit Bureau,

After receiving a copy of my credit report, I have found incorrect information reported.

My account at XYZ, account #111111, was paid in full as agreed and not a charge-off. Please remove this.

I never paid Kelly Co. 60 days late. Account #12344. Please correct this.

This Tax Lien Docket #555555 was paid in full. I do not owe this.

My name is John Doe, and I reside at 2233 Park Avenue, Any Town, California 22222. My social security number is 111-22-3333. My previous address was 6143 Summer Lane, Any Town, California 22222. My birthdate is 11-17-50.

Sincerely,
John Doe

With this information, your determination and a little patience, you too can

Be Creditwize!